My cover was inspired by the life of King David. He was a man after God's heart. He was a mighty warrior for the Lord and then he found his self running for his life.
King Saul was seeking to kill him. He found refuge in a cave. The cave was his place of refuge. In this place we can call on God and he will deliver. David did and he was delivered.

Later in his life, David had family problems. He had a daughter that was raped by her half brother. It left her disgraced, empty and unwanted. This act he called love.

He said he loved her so much he could not live without her. So he made himself sick so she could come and take care of him and he violently raped her, after that he hated, and put her out in the street and shut the door. These great stories can be found in 1&2 Samuel in the Bible

I was comforted because it is true there is nothing new under the sun.

IT'S TIME OUT FOR HIDING

FOR HIDING

CATHERINE COOPER

Ordering Information:

For orders and inquiries, please contact:
1-888-404-1388
www.goldtouchpress.com
book.order@goldtouchpress.com

Printed in the United States of America

CONTENTS

The Acknowledged Page

First I thank the Lord Jesus Christ,
who gave me inspiration and direction.

My church family: they mean everything to me.
I love and appreciate each of you.
No matter what part you played you
have made me live again.

I am so thankful to each of you. You helped through your prayer's
and encouragement.
God always had a brother or a sister in my corner. Thanks

My loving husband: Minister,
Michael Cornelius Cooper.
He is my best friend. He is the most loving husband.
The Lord made him just for me. Thank you, Jesus.
We have learned how to become one, love, laugh and enjoy each
other everyday. He makes me laugh everyday.

Thanks to these people who have worked as a mighty force of God
in the flesh to help and nourish
"the word works" in me.
They are here to see the end result of all their preaching,
teaching, praying and fasting has not been in vain.
They have trained me to live for
Jesus with my whole heart.

They love unconditionally that agape love.
Thank you Jesus for: Pastor Anthony L. Speight and
Sis Revondolyn E. Speight.
A special appreciation to:

Sis. Padrika Gray who has been an inspiration to me,
she helped me with my cover design and editing.
Thanks you taking me to the next level.
To my children whom I love so much.
They have encouraged
me all the way in finishing this book.
Juanita thanks for all your patience,
she did some editing too.

INTRODUCTION

Inside this book is the story of my life. I had a pretend face. I had decided if nobody really knew me and they didn't know my past, then I could just live for now and if I don't tell, they won't know. So, for 32 years I never told anyone; but I was a mess. I lived in fear, defeated, suspicious of everyone and everything that was good. I thought everybody wanted something from me. I had silent anger, a roller coaster lifestyle; today life is good and tomorrow it is the end of the world. But I didn't want that to happen yet because I wasn't ready, and worst, I couldn't get ready. I lived with fear all of my life, real and imaginary, loneliness, mood swings, because of the things I suffered as a child. I was an emotional wreck, but God set me free and I am here to tell others.

The purpose of this book is to bring deliverance to someone; the people of God who have been called at this hour to come out of their dark places and be healed—totally set free. Yes, all kinds of people have suffered fears caused by things that happened in their life, and it's time to let them know it was not their fault that they are suffering today. After you read and study this book, you will be set free just like me. The time is now to come out and live your life like never before. I will describe the hiding places we run to when we are hurt, feel abandoned, or need to feel safe; but in the end there is no place to hide. The only safe place is in the arms of Jesus. Psalms 17:8 "Keep me as the apple of the eye, hide me under the shadow of thy wings." I am here to tell you that because of Jesus, there is safety and comfort in my new life; and I want to share this with as many people as I can reach. This book is not limited to any age, race, gender, or nationality; it's not just for those who are living in an emotional cage, but for those who feel free. Teenagers have experienced abuse, rape, and have been molested, as well as adults. They all need to be healed and set free. The complete healing will come instantly. God has assured me this will take place. He did it to me, so I have first hand experience of what God can do if we are willing to go all the way with him. Sometimes it might feel like you are walking blind—not able to see anything around you; but God is faithful, and he said He would be a light in our path. So, look up and live.

When this healing takes place, there will be no evidence that the enemy ever had a hold on you, and that is how God works. Recently, I remember trying to look back to find where the enemy was, but I was only able to see victory. Once you have gone through the trial that God has allowed in your life, he will say it is finished. You will know it is finished and there will never be enough devils to take you backwards. I have finally moved forward and I am not going back. My prayer is that you will believe and let God do it for you too. I hope I will be able to express what God is telling me to share with you, so the results will be just as He said. I am praying, "Not my will, but God's will be done."

A FINISHED WORK!!

Note:

As you read, you will notice that some incidents and situations throughout this book are being repeated. This is not due to confusion as to where they should be placed within the chapters. These incidents have been repeated to help you see the amount of confusion and "repeated" emotional trauma that children experience, as they recall painful events and persistently try to make sense out of what has happened, or is happening to them, from a child's perspective.

My Story

My name is Catherine Cooper. Today, I am here to tell you a true story; it goes like this: Back in a time when things were simpler than now, people were trusting; you could entrust your children into their hands. You could leave your home and not think about someone breaking in. There were no burglar alarms. We all were safe; we just knew it, or were we?

I was a little girl that knew she was safe at home with her three sisters and her mother. On the outside, everything looked normal. I was the third child and I was happy. Then one day, I was home taking a bath. Here comes the enemy; he was setting the stage for the rest of my life. I was playing in the tub, as little girls do. All of a sudden, there was a person that I knew standing in the doorway. "Surprise, I came to see how you were doing today," he said. "Fine," I said and kept on playing. Then he was gone. Just as I got out of the tub, he came back. "Oh, you're so pretty," he said, as he gave me a touch where later there would be breasts, and he walked away. I just kept on doing what I was doing. I didn't think anything of it. Here comes my sister, so we begin to play and I forgot about what happened; I said nothing about it to anyone.

Well, the enemy was testing me, but I didn't know it (that's what he relies on, your lack of knowledge) so there wasn't any fear at that point. Now, the enemy is wondering, "Will she tell?" I didn't say a word to anybody, and the games began. In those days, children didn't talk to adults or express themselves about things to adults, the way they do today.

The stage was set. He showed up at bath time, even on the times my sister and I were together; but he didn't come in. He would just let us know he was there. When I was alone, he would come in and tell me how good I smelled, give a little touch here and there, and he would leave. He would go downstairs and act like nothing happened. After this happened several times, I started getting scared; but who was I going to tell? He would always be upstairs when I was alone, and he would tell me nobody was going to believe me anyway. He would say things like, "that powder smells good on you; I bet it tastes good too." After I heard that, I stopped putting on powder after my baths, thinking he would leave me alone. But that didn't work. By now the fear and intimidation were in place, and it would take me years to get over it; but the worst was yet to come. I thought if I took my bath with my sister, I would never have to be alone. I was only setting myself up to be dependent on others, but I needed someone else to protect me or to at least be with me at all times.

Nighttime wasn't a good time for me, because now he was playing mind games. Late at night he would hurt my mom and we would awake to hear her screaming in pain. For a child that was frightening. They were in bed together; is that the way it should be? The fear was really working on me. I was always wondering what he was doing to her, but the next day they acted as if nothing had happened.

I remember my older sister and the pain he caused her. My mom was out of town. She left us with friends, because our grandmother was sick. My sister went home to clean up before mom got home from her trip, she was asleep looked up and he was home, he attacked her. He had been out of town, but had come home early. He was supposed to get home later that day, to pick mom up from the airport. Two of us were together with another family. The two older sister were together with our neighbors which was right next door to our house. We were on our way home when we saw police cars near our house. We kept walking. The closer we got, the more we knew those police cars were at our house. We ran to see what was happening. We got closer to one of the police cars and he was in the back seat. So, we ran in the house to see what was going on. When I stepped in the door, I saw my sister balled up in the corner, crying and shaking. The police were trying to make us go back outside. She was beaten up, with scratches on her face and neck. Her clothes were torn off and she was holding them on with her hand. She was in the corner and all she kept saying was, "I came over to clean up and I fell asleep on the couch." I looked around the room and there was blood on the floor, and spots of blood leading to the front door.

After the police left, panic hit us. Mom was on her way home. We had to get that house cleaned up now! They took him to jail and now there was no one to pick her up from the airport. What a surprise she had waiting on her! We were afraid that when she got home, she would say it was our fault. Mom was mad when she got home; she never even looked at her, she just got busy trying to get him back home. She got the keys to her car and left us home. All day long we were quiet and scared. Finally, she came back home and said, "Come on." We did not know where we were going. It never entered our minds that we were going to the police station, but we picked him up and went home like nothing ever happened. We were quite scared, and just went to our rooms upstairs for the rest of the day. No one said a word, not aloud anyway. Our home became like a quiet prison. In our own ways, each of us began a cycle of destruction. I began to seek friends away from home; anybody I could go and stay with so I would not have to stay at home with him. The silence was killing us. We never knew where the attack was coming from, or when it would hit. He worked out of town; he drove moving trucks long distance. While he was gone, we spent that time preparing an escape route for ourselves. It was like preparing for a hurricane to hit, but not knowing for sure when or where. All my life I lived expecting something bad to happen. If something good happened, I thought "Look out, the hit is coming." It was almost like the calm before the storm. He would always get home from work in the middle of the night, when we were asleep, and when we awoke that morning, we would see him laying there in bed asleep. Now, the fear was alive again. We would tip toe through the house, nobody would make a sound, careful not to awaken him.

I fell in love with school, not for education, but because it was my means of escape. In school I was shy and didn't talk much, so the kids didn't know my problems. The girls didn't like me and the boys did. I tried to stay from them, but, the boys were the only ones who would say anything to me. I was pretty with long hair and fair skin, so the girls always said, "She thinks she's cute." Then they would want to fight me for no reason. There was one girl that talked to me, and we began to spend all our time together. I stayed at her house all the time. We were together every day; I needed her and she needed me. Her father had just killed her mother, and I was there for her; I believed she would be there for me also. My mom didn't like her or our new friendship, because she had brothers, six of them; but that didn't matter to me. We didn't see them anyway. Our friendship was an issue to me, because I needed to be needed by someone at that time, plus it kept me away from home and I felt safe. It seemed as if things were going great. Our friendship allowed me to get away from home, and my friend was getting over the loss of her mother, with my help. We trusted each other with our deepest feelings, but that area was getting ready to be tested.

There we were, two sick people trying to heal each other. Then, one day I went to her house and she took me downstairs to their basement. It was dark and cold, and I asked why we were there. "Oh, my brother wants to see you," she said. Little did I know there were five other guys with him. He grabbed me and pulled me in a room, and they took turns raping me. They were saying and doing all kinds of nasty things to me, and I couldn't tell anyone about it. I felt nasty. Maybe it was my fault; I kept telling myself I should have known better. Now I couldn't go to her house anymore, so I stayed in my room with no friends—alone again. I couldn't tell my sister; it was just too nasty to tell anyone. What would my sister think of me? Then, three days later my friend came to visit me, and I just acted as if nothing was wrong. I had to pretend I was all-right, because I needed a friend; it was better than nothing.

Now the summer was coming. I remember we were going to North Carolina to stay with our dad. The night before we were planning to leave, my mother was all exited, and we were packing. She called me downstairs and said, "Come on your going to the store to get some clothes." I was afraid. "I don't want to go," I kept saying. But Mom said, "Yes you are going." I begged and cried. Well, I was always crying, but she said go! So I left crying, and we got in the car. I tried to get my sister to go with me, but momma said no! I got in the car and sat still as I could, afraid to breathe. We got to the store, a big store like Wal-Mart, with a big parking lot. He was driving toward the back of the lot. I was as far over in the seat as possible. The doors were locked and I couldn't get out. I looked for the lock, but was too scared to scream or move. It was dark and just the little lamp from the street was on. He stopped the car and said, "You belong to me." I cried and cried, but he said "Be quiet, no one will hear you." Then he grabbed me and started kissing me. It was so nasty. He took off his belt and I began pushing him back. He grabbed my hand and pulled it behind me. He took the belt and tied me up and began to rape me in the car—the same man, my mother's boyfriend! When it was over, he took me in the store, bought me clothes and said, "Don't tell; no one will believe you anyway." I was in so much pain. I remember I could hardly walk without hurting. We got back home. I was crying again. I cried from Connecticut to New Jersey, where we met my father. Over the years, the devil continued to plant seeds of fear, intimidation, mistrust, low self-esteem and destructive emotions into my life. The rest of my story will tell you how God has worked in my life to change, uproot, and to replant faith, trust, confidence, and love; it has been a long journey.

The Place

Have you ever been riding by a place, looking at it from the outside, but in your mind, you could imagine good things going on in that place? In your mind, you could see joy being shared, the family would be laughing, playing, and singing together. Well, that was on television; because in my place it was cold, damp, secluded and dark. This was my "hiding place." It was in a "vision" that God showed me where I lived and where I became the person that I was. He showed me a dark "cave". There was warmth on the outside, sunshine, green grass and flowers; but once you step inside the cave there is another view with the atmosphere of danger. It is cold, dark, and damp inside there. The deeper you go inside the cave, the colder and darker it gets. It was almost like the darkness of a tomb.

But right now, I am at a time in my life that doing all I can for God is first and foremost. I look for God everywhere I go and in everything I am doing; in my mind, nothing is too hard for God. It took me a lot of years to get to this place. Now the Lord is dealing with me about all the times I ran away so I wouldn't have to face my problems. We run when we get hurt, because we don't want anyone to see us—because we are embarrassed.

Embarrassment makes a person feel awkward or ashamed, and makes children unable to play. When a person goes into hiding, they are trying to keep out of sight, trying to conceal their secrets, trying to retreat to a safe place. As a child, I had to find places to hide. My place was outside my room window where we had a basement built. It was built like a little house attached to our main house, so it had a separate roof, and on the roof of this basement, outside my room window is where I slept at night to hide and try to keep myself safe. I got comfortable with this place. I stayed out there, away from the house, under my own blanket of stars, moon and sky. Out there I felt safe, because he couldn't find me there without giving himself away. It was a place to keep myself safe, because no one else was trying to keep me safe. I decided that if he didn't see me, he couldn't hurt me again.

Learning How To Hide

Thinking back on my childhood, I remember I would say, "If you can't see me, then you can't hurt me." But when you hide you can get lost; the real you gets lost. If a child never gets to learn who they are, there will always be a void in that child's life—an emptiness that will always need to be filled. When a person hides for too long, sometimes they cannot find their way back. As a child, I learned to pretend and most children do live in a fantasyland at one time or another. For me, hiding in my fantasyland became my way of escape and I got real good at it. I lived a lie every day. I had to pretend that things were fine and nothing was going on. Where there is hiding, there is also the spirit of fear. Fear is a heavy load for a child to carry. It is amazing how a child can learn to adapt to the fear of the devil when they have to run, hide, and don't tell. Once that seed is planted, it is easy to learn to fear, but hard to get rid of it. On a daily basis I had to pretend that things were just fine, that I enjoyed being with certain people, and that we were a happy family—a normal family. Soon you begin to think that pretending is normal. You tell yourself that everybody lives like this. A male family member said we were lucky because he was there taking care of us. My mother thought she was doing what was best, but little did she know I was living in constant fear and hatred. I lived in fear every day of my life not knowing what would happen from one day to the next, and hating to go home. I tried to stay away from home as much as possible. I had to pretend that I liked this man, in front of my mother and sisters. He came and went daily, as if nothing ever happened. Sometimes he would catch me upstairs by myself, and he would try to feel on me and tell me I was doing a good job or something. I would get away from him by calling my sister, and when he saw her coming, he would let me go. The only time I could breath easy was when he went out of town on business for his job. The fear of him was built in me, and each time I ran away from home as a child, I learned all the things that were contrary to the Word of God. When other young girls were looking for other things in life, I was learning how to hide and to escape. I spent many nights awake, listening to my mother hollering at the hands of the same man. He was my mother's way out of welfare—her support, but he was my nightmare. Many nights I thought of ways to get rid of him, but I didn't want to go to jail, so one more time I ran away from home at the age of 13 years old. I had nowhere to go, so I took a chance and went to my real father. A new change, a new way of life, I hoped. However, I was still not able to tell anyone the reason I left. I was still hiding. I had to hide while I was away from home because if I said or did the wrong thing, it might open up a can of worms and cause a lot of questions. I could not trust anyone, or any man, because they might be the same as the one I ran away from. He told me if I said anything, no one would believe me anyway, and he knew where I was at all times. It seemed like everywhere I went, he was there.

Hiding became my life and the real me got lost. For so many years I didn't know who I was or what I should have been in life. I had no goals. Just to make it to the next day was good enough for me. Confidence, I had none. Self-worth, I had none. Praise God he kept my mind. Somebody, somewhere had to be praying for me, and my sisters too.

God Had A Plan

As a little girl, I loved God and our family was involved with church. It was our life. I remember standing on a box to sing in the choir and being baptized at 4 years old. Then my mother gave me to my great aunt and my great grandmother. They raised me and taught me to love God. Our family was into everything in the church. We were cooking; some of us were in the choir; my uncle was a deacon. We ate at the pastor's home on Sunday. Many times, my aunt would leave early for church, and leave me with my uncle so he could bring me later. Every little girl loves to take pictures, because it makes them feel pretty. But at the age of six years old, my uncle started taking naked pictures of me. He had on no clothes and he told me, "Don't tell nobody; they won't believe you anyway." Because my great grandmother was considered the "mother of the church," on the outside everything looked fine—the perfect family, but on the dark side of things there were many family secrets.

For about thirty years I blocked these things out. I asked God to set me free because there are a lot of hurting people out there. But then I asked God, "What can I do for them?" "I am nobody." God told me, "Yes, you are somebody; you are a royal priesthood." I had to learn to accept what the Word said about me, not what I feel or think of myself. Well, I decided no more hiding! It's time to come out and be set free. The devil was planting seeds of destruction in my life at an early age. Why? Because I was anointed by God for a specific purpose. The devil knew that I was anointed, but I didn't. This is what he was trying to stop from the beginning. The devil knows the Word of God, but he believes that we do not. He tried to destroy me before I ever went to school for the first time. He was afraid of God's plan, so he started early. When I see little children being abused early in life, I know it is only because God has a plan. Even though the devil tries to delay our calling, he cannot stop the plans God has for us, and that is what this book is about. It is to let everyone know the devil cannot stop anything that God said you can have or be in life. If God says it is yours, then go and get it. I pray it won't take as long for you to get there, as it took for me. That is why I am talking about it to everyone who will listen.

The Lord told me that while I am pouring myself out, I am continually being healed. When you spend a lot of your time hiding so you won't get hurt, you miss-out on life and you learn not to trust people. I felt that the ones that should have protected me had betrayed me, and they let me down. My mother, my aunt, and my great grandmother didn't do their job, so that left me incomplete and afraid.

MORE CHILDHOOD TROUBLES

I remember at one point in my life, at an early age, the devil tried to draw me into a lifestyle of lesbianism. I had a cousin at my uncle's house in South Carolina. During the day she was a normal friendly girl; we played together and had fun. But I was afraid of her at night; plus, there was no electricity and no indoor bathroom, so I had to go outside in the dark to use the toilet. I was always afraid when the sun would start going down. I would ball up into the fetal position and I had a habit of rocking myself to sleep. My cousin would get in the bed with me and begin to kiss me on the mouth, and to feel all over my body. I would be paralyzed at that point because I was already afraid. She put her tongue in my mouth and I would gag, because it was just so nasty, and I felt so unclean. I was glad when it was time to leave to go back home. However, when I got back home, my nasty uncle, the well-respected deacon in the church, was there. The only comfort I had was my great grandmother. She loved me and took care of me in the daytime.

I also grew up in a violent and alcoholic home. Other people would come over and drink, and I was always hiding. They all called me the cry baby, because I cried all the time. If someone would yell at me, I would cry. Another devastation came when I met my father for the first time. I was in the sixth grade when I met him. He came to visit some of his family who lived in Virginia, where I was at the time. I didn't know that their family hated our family. Anyway, he came to our house and said, "Hi Cathy, don't you know me?" Well of course I didn't, so I said "No." He said, "I am your daddy." I was shocked and started crying. My great grandmother was there for me and she assured me that he was my daddy. So I went back to meet him. When I was Eleven and a-half years old, my daddy wanted to take us shopping. He had my older sister with him.She lived with my grandmother, but we never saw or talked to each other until my mom would come to Virginia. My younger sister lived with our mom, and she would be with mom when they came to Virginia to visit. I used to think she was so lucky to live with mom. They always seemed so happy when they were traveling. I remember my mom had a convertible top car that looked like so much fun to ride in. My mom never even asked if I wanted to go home with her though. I would see mom maybe twice a year, always Easter and Christmas. Mom never brought me anything and never asked if I wanted to be with her. I thought it would be so much fun. She lived in the big city of New York, but she would come to visit and leave without me.

Anyway, back to my dad. He wanted to go and get my other sister, who lived in Virginia, to go shopping with us. That day I had two sisters and one dad, and his new wife with me. It was like I was meeting my family for the first time. My sister had a rough life with alcoholism, cursing, and fighting; that is how her life was different from ours. Even though we lived in a (so-called) Christian family, and my grandfather was a deacon in the church. His wife was one of the mothers of the church. What went on behind closed doors, I do not know, but I have seen some of the fruit of that tree. I know she has had a troubled life, but God is going to save her so that she can tell of His wondrous works also. Those things are taking place as I write this. I pray for the angels of the Lord to protect her life and the Lord to spare her soul.

I have new information since I wrote this, my sister went to be with the Lord and I need to let you know that the Lord honored my prayer. I had an opportunity to share with her the joy of receiving forgiveness by Jesus Christ. It changed my life. One day our mother got very sick and was in the hospital, my sister and I were with her but for some reason my sister couldn't sit still so she just got up and left the room. I went after her to see what was wrong and as we began to talk, she began to share with me that as she was sitting there looking at our mother all she could see is my mom telling her, as they were riding in the car one day, I wish you were never born. She felt that I was better than her and she didn't need to be there. The spirit of unworthiness had taken over her life. So I shared with her it was only by the grace of God that I am the way that I am. I'm not better I'm just forgiven. I have lived some of the same things that she's lived. At that time she was living in a hotel and I told her that I too lived in a hotel with all six of my children and had no place to go. So my life was no different than hers and never have I ever thought I was better than her, I love her just the way she was. The Lord showed me as I was talking to her that she was like a bird in a cage flying from one side to the other continuously hitting her head. So he directed me to open the door and let her out. And we prayed right outside the hospital. She told me she was coming back upstairs so I left her there. As she entered the room, all of the family was there, and she had a smile on her face. She didn't look like the same person that had left the room. The family members one by one kept asking her what happen to you, you don't look the same. I let her know as she forgave our mother that God would forgive her and teach her how to forgive herself. She needed to forgive herself, why because we have so much guilt that we carry around. As we forgive ourselves it no longer matters what other people say or do.

Proverbs 17:22 A cheerful heart is good medicine, but a crusted spirit dries up the bones.

Proverbs 15:13 A happy heart makes the face cheerful, but heartache crushes the spirit.

When abuse is introduced into your life it creates a destructive attitude or behavior in you. You know that your attitude controls everything about you. "Attitude before ability" is what my Pastor has always taught us. And because of my attitude I couldn't receive what he was trying to say. Years later I began to seek for a change and it had to start with the way I thought about myself and every situation in my life. How you think is how you will live, act or talk. You can be positive or negative sometimes both at the same time. But the words you say comes from within, you think it first then say it(attitude). The biggest thing we go thru is the blame game, that's an attitude, or the justified attitude-- I'm like this because of what happened to me as a child. So there's an attitude adjustment that is needed and that comes from God. He can change everything about you, old things become new and all things are passed away once we repent. If there's no constructive attention toward the abuse the destructive behavior will continue to grow and as you get older, life got worst as years continued to come and go. You even lose track of time. As life passes you by, you miss out on things people take for granted. Like just hanging out with friends having fun laughing, playing games. It's alonely life, because you can't let your guard down for one minute.

Moving To Connecticut

Months went by and my mom finally answered that silent plea that I had cried, to live with her. I didn't know what lied ahead. She came and got us and myself. Well, by this time they were beautiful, light-skinned teenage girls with long hair. All the other girls in school didn't like us. I remember thinking there must be something I am doing wrong, because none of the girls in this new school in Connecticut liked me. They would pick fights with me; we had to fight every day to get home from school. Two or three girls would just jump me. They said they did it because I thought I was cute. They would pull out our hair, try to cut us up with razors, and they would try to mess up our faces with scratches. Thanks be to God, they never did—but they sure did try. I was jumped one day while going to the bus stop, which was in the middle of downtown in Stanford, Connecticut. All kinds of people were out there and no one would help me. They rubbed my face on the ground and said, "We'll show you; you think you are cute." After that, I began carrying a razor knife with me. By this tine, I was 13 or 14 years old, but I was going to be bad now and defend myself.

But when my sisters and myself got home, we would be fighting each other. Remember, one sister was raised in a home with that lifestyle. My mom would go to work and come home. Her boyfriend also lived with us. He loved the idea of having all those females to choose from. At night he would be with my mom. All of our rooms were connected together, so we could hear what was going on in their room. He would hurt her and we could hear her crying after he finished. She would tell him he was hurting her, and he wouldn't say a word. Later, I believe he used that to frighten me. All the boys liked us (me and my sisters), but the girls didn't. That is another trick the devil uses against young teenage girls. It makes you feel that if only the boys like you, then that is a good thing; but what you end up getting is a reputation, even if you haven't done anything. The boys would say you might as well do it, because everybody says you have. For as long as I can remember, family members have always called us whores, all our lives. They would tell us our daddy was no good, and we won't be any good either. Nobody had anything good to say about us, except how cute we were.

The feeling of being pretty should be a good thing. Everybody wants to be pretty, well not me, it only got me in trouble. It was a spirit that was driving me to another place of hiding. People would say 'you are pretty', and I would want to do is run and hide. Being called pretty was something negative for me, when I became an adult I hated people to say 'you are so pretty'. I would just try to play it off because I didn't have the confidence to believe I was pretty and that was a good thing as a child it brought pain and shame to me. I was attacked because I was pretty, either sexual or physical. Why is that important because if you don't like your self how can you really love someone else. The things that happed in my life in school as a child helped develop what type of adult I would become. That's the reason the enemy attacks children early in life. He knows who you are if you don't.

As an adult I tried to forget my childhood but I spent a good number of years trying to do the opposite of the way I was raised. Some good children try to do everything bad trying to prove they're not good. Bad children can also spend some time trying to prove that they are good but as soon as the rejection comes it triggers something and causes them to revert. Like me, it still existed inside waiting to come out. It does cause you to revert even as a Christian, because as the trigger comes your victory is gone; but there is hope in the word.

Forgiveness is the first step; *forgive those who have trespassed against you, that you might be forgiven of your trespasses. Mark 11:25*

LEARNING HOW TO LOVE

Love means: "to lean on; to give and to receive from; to trust, admire; beloved; show deep affection," that is the meaning from the dictionary. Now, let me give you my definition of love before God healed me: "to love meant to smile and keep right on going; to hurry up and get by; don't get involved; don't get too close; sit back and wish you can have something; admire from a distance; let no one in; protect at all costs."

God had to teach me to trust; he had to teach me what real love was all about, and today I am able to love people without question. When the Lord was teaching me about real love I wept like a baby, because of the revelation the Lord showed me. God brought change to my life with that new outlook on love. That was one of the many changes God would make in me before my complete deliverance could take place. Learning to love was a process that I had to go through.

SAVED AND STILL HIDING

I had drawn an imaginary line that I could not let anyone cross; and I mean no one, not even my husband. When things got to that line, we just didn't talk about it—we didn't go there. Again, I decided if I let no one in, I wouldn't get hurt. As long as no one came over that imaginary line then I was fine— that was my "safety net". But once someone crossed that line, it was time to hide again; time to go home and stay there. If no one called to check on me, that made me mad. If someone called, then that made me mad also. My husband said, "I can't do right for trying; what do you want?" I didn't know, so I as unable to express what I needed. For many years I was unable to express my feelings. I just wouldn't say anything. I would just go with the flow, but not be happy. I was just existing; not expecting anything; hoping one day it will all be over. This mind-set followed me right over into my salvation.

After salvation, it took years of applying my pastor's teachings and the teachings of the Holy Ghost, to make me the person I am today. Not that I am perfect or do not make mistakes now, but God is still working on me, perfecting me. As a child, I learned to hide and pretend, and then I got lost and could not find my way out. I lived a lie every day, and with so many years of practice, by the time I became an adult, I was good at it.

CHARACTERISTICS OF A HIDING PERSON

The number one characteristic of a hiding person is FEAR. We have all experienced fear somewhere in our lives. This kind of fear is a "panic" that comes over you. It paralyzes you because you are always on your guard, fearing that your secrets are going to be found out. There is never a time to relax, and it doesn't matter who you are with, you cannot relax. This fear is tormenting; the devil walks in at will and never lets up. He continually talks to you and because it is a familiar voice, you listen to him. He is always telling you that everybody is after you and nobody likes you. This keeps you still; immobilized in one place; too scared to move; too scared to ask for help. The devil tells you that people do not understand you and they do not believe what you say; and anyway, who do you think you are to tell anybody anything? Even in writing this book, the devil tried to tell me nobody is going to buy it. But you know? That doesn't matter, because God told me to write it. And even if nobody buys it, I am being obedient to God; and after talking to my covering (my pastor and his wife), it doesn't matter what the devil says anymore.

Another characteristic of a hiding person is mood swings. Mood swings are marked changes in a person's temperament, like from euphoric (joyful or excited) to depression (extreme sadness or despair). Have you ever been somewhere just having a good time, and all of a sudden, you notice the person you are with is not talking or laughing anymore? They are just kind of sitting there, and their mind is miles away from you. You ask the person what is the matter, and they say,

"Nothing." You can tell something is wrong, but the other person won't open up to you, so you just ignore them. It seems the person doesn't want to talk to you, so you leave them alone. In a little while, you see that same person laughing again, but with somebody else, and you cannot figure it out. So you label them as a "funny acting person". Or, maybe you were having a good time with a person, and suddenly they were ready to go, right now, with no explanation, and just got angry for no good reason. I wasn't the arguing type, but I would get real quiet for no good reason. I would go for days without speaking to anyone.

The worst part of it all is that there is a war going on inside of you. Part of me would want to talk while the other side says "no".

There are so many more mood swings, like depression, having anxiety attacks so bad that you can't breathe. Sometimes people get so afraid we hide within ourselves and just miss out on life. I remember not too many years ago I was going to a doctor and he would tell me 'you are so tense, you need to relax'. I said, 'I am relaxed', and he showed me how tense I was just by touching me. I was automatically unaware of how tense I was, I had been this way so for so long it was just the way I was. That's just how fast they happened, in a split second It takes a good awareness of yourself at all times, because anything can be a trigger. But the Bible say's we have control over our spirits. I had been hiding for so long that only I could break the spirit that was over me. The Holy Ghost will teach you, but you must put into action what you've been taught.

A wise man fears the Lord, and shuns evil: but a fool is hot headed and reckless Proverbs 1:16

The biggest thing we go thru is the blame game or it's an attitude or a state of justification, saying things like, 'this happened because this happen to me when I was a child'. When I was a child I thought as a child, now that I'm a women I thinks as a woman.

Professional Hider

A professional hider is that person who has learned how to hide very well, from an early age. If you are a professional hider, the devil has trained you well to put on your face and move straight through a crowd of people as if everything is fine, and you believe no one will see you. But let someone cross the line with you, like a waitress at a restaurant who tries to tell you something, or make a suggestion to you; all of a sudden, something inside of you says, "Why is she telling me what to do?" "Doesn't she know who I am?" It is an attitude that takes over you. It is a familiar spirit. You don't rebuke it because it has always been there. The devil planted a seed in you. He planted an attitude that says, "I am somebody and she is not recognizing me." In a way, you want to be recognized, but on the other hand, you don't. There is a battle going on in you. Yes and no, at the same time, is going on in your mind.

Professional hiders are people who are walking in fear, they are pretenders. Pretenders are fake and live their life as a lie, they get lost and believe themselves to be something they really aren't. You can be a business person working on the same job everyday for years; with the same people but never really letting anyone get to know the real you or what has happened to you. I remember when I was working in the beauty salon and I had worked there for years with the same ladies; One day The Oprah Winfrey show was just coming on the air so everybody looked forward to watching it daily, me too. This one show came on and a young girl was having trouble with her family but she never told them what was wrong. The family was trying to find out what to do with her. The young girl just began to cry, and then burst out and said she had been molested by her mom's boyfriend. I was sitting there and all of a sudden it seemed as if a spotlight was shining on me I wanted to run and hide but I couldn't I was working on someone's hair. What was worst than that was listening to the opinions of everybody else that were watching the program. They were all blaming the girl, look at her, look how she's dressed, she so fast. I wanted to scream out it's not her fault but I kept working, than Oprah began to talk and to me it sounded like she was agreeing with them, like it was actually the girl's fault. The young girl was crying and no one wanted to comfort her. At last I couldn't take it anymore I began to defend the girl and everybody was looking at me like I was crazy. A lady in the salon said, 'how do you know', and before I knew it I said, 'because that's what happened to me and I didn't do anything'. I was embarrassed; I didn't know how I could go back to work there, because they know my secret now. I didn't know it at the time, but one of the ladies in the salon was a rape crisis worker. The next day that lady came back and I saw her, I thought she was there to see her stylist so I let her know that her stylist wasn't there. She said, 'actually I came to see you'. I want to talk to you about yesterday. I was so afraid; I have seen this lady every week for years and didn't want to share this with her . She told me she works with victims' everyday and she never would have guessed that I had been through anything like that. She asked if I had been through a counseling program, I said no. She wanted me to come to the center and talk, at that time I still wasn't ready to come out. My first thoughts were my children and my husband; they didn't know any of this about me. She told me that I was in such good shape compared to the other people she saw everyday. She actually wanted ME to come and talk to the other people. I didn't think I had it in me so I made up excuses and never went. At that time I wasn't ready to come out of my cave.

I said all of that to show how well we can hide and blend in as normal.

The Controlled Hider

The controlled hider is controlled by emotions only. The wife who has been yelled at by the husband, who tells her what to do over and over, she is reminded of the harsh control that her dad had over her. It is almost like going backwards to the days that dad yelled at her because she did something wrong and she could not say anything to him. Now she can't say anything, or express her feelings to her husband. She can act normal until the children do something wrong, and when they do, she takes her hidden anger out on them. She may even vent her anger on a stranger at the store or another child that cannot say anything back. It is like a charge that goes off in your head; something says let me loose so I can go after them, and the release feels good. It feels like the red stop light has just turned green, and now you can go. You loose that spirit on almost everyone you come in contact with, chewing them up and spitting them out as you go. In public you will try to control that wild emotion, but you only end up belittling or ignoring the person, maybe treating them as if they do not know their job, or something else mean. The people you have chewed up and spit out are trying to figure out what just happened, and they are feeling bad. You have managed to make them feel what you are feeling; now you are waiting on the next customer, and the cycle continues on. But there is peace for your spirit. It is Jesus Christ. He will supply you with all the peace you need.

John14:27 Jesus said I am leaving you with a gift- peace of mind and heart. And the peace I give is a gift the world cannot give. So don't be troubled or afraid".

I desired to have peace in my life, but I couldn't get a grip on letting go to get the peace I needed. I couldn't take the chance of letting someone find out that I wasn't what I appeared to be on the outside. I had to control everything in my life; it made my world pretty small. The goals and aspirations I wanted to achieve seemed too far out of reach thus making it impossible to see myself making anything out of myself. All of that is against the word of God; those ideas will keep you in your cave for years to come. I remember when I received that peace, I was at a conference and the instructions were to be quiet and receive the spirit of peace. Well I wanted to see what was going on but we were up high in the church and the speaker said ,shh shh, and I could see the spirit moving and every time someone would make noise I saw the cloud stop, when it got quiet again the cloud began to move again. That day I received the gift and it was just as the word said only God could give it to me.

Philippians. 4:7 and the peace of God, which suppresses all understanding, will guard your hearts and minds through Christ Jesus.

THE SUPER CHRISTIAN

This is the person that is saved and nothing bothers them. "I just quote the word and I am delivered. I never need prayer. I am just saved and mad about it." Of course, this doesn't apply to every Christian that is confident and exercises their faith. If it applies to you, you will know it. You are mad because the devil is telling you, "If you weren't saved, then you could release some of that pressure." The pressure is on you and you cannot let your guard down for a minute, or someone will find you out. The guard I am talking about is the fact that you think the devil cannot hurt you, because you are hiding behind the Word. But in reality, the Word has become a shield against yourself. You are always praying and quoting scripture, but you are not yielding yourself before God. You never show any love, you are always judgmental and critical of things. There is something wrong with this picture.

You are the type of person that makes people run away from you. It's because of your critical spirit, in which you like to see the wrong in everybody else but yourself. You become self righteous, and there are times that you don't know exactly what God wants from you, but you act as if you know what he wants from every body else. If you keep busy trying to change everybody else, then you won't have time to work on yourself. I found that every time God wanted to deal with me about something the enemy would make sure someone with that same problem came my way. So now I can fix them and that would make me feel better, because I'm doing the will of God. But I didn't love or care about their soul; I just wanted to show the devil that I was saved. I was praying but not taking the time to listen to God. I prayed asking for help, but walked away before God could tell me anything, but I prayed and that was what I was supposed to do. Until I got a real relationship with God I didn't get any results. A relationship works both ways; give and take. **Pray, listen and then obey**.

I knew nothing about the fruits of the spirit. Love, joy, peace, long-suffering goodness, meekness and the greatest of these is love. I needed Love so bad, real love (agape love).

The Marriage And
Sex Life Of A Hider

All little girls think about their wedding day. There is something wonderful and exciting about getting married. I have had the privilege of being in a couple of weddings, and indeed I've learned a lot by being involved. As I listened to the pre-marital counseling, I began to realize what was missing in my marriage; but by the grace of God, He made up for the missing parts as we went through our tests and trials together. Some of those tests and trials were very hard, but God knew just what we could bear. I thank God for all that he has done in our marriage. It seems like God knew what to allow in our lives, and just how much pressure to apply—He has done a complete work.

When we say our wedding vows, we expect only the best as we go into the journey of our lives together. But because my husband didn't know my past, he had no way of knowing what he was in for. For example: not many people anticipate that the person they are marrying is going to be sick one day, so they don't really prepare for that. I believe God designed it this way from the beginning of time. When I got married, all I could believe was that Michael loved me and I could not even imagine myself with anyone else. God has given us a lot of grace and mercy, and I am so thankful for that. Our marriage is even stronger today.

One of the problems in our marriage was because of the fact we got married so young. Everybody kept saying it won't last, they are too young, but we loved each other and had all intentions to stay together. With God, we did. Things were good on the surface. I really did love him, but sex was something I could live without. I didn't need sex, but we all know that men cannot live without it. Because I felt this way, the enemy tried hard to make me feel unworthy. That was a real battle in my mind. Every night was a battle zone I didn't want to face. I spent many years in fear that my husband would leave me, because the devil would torment me and tell me things like: I was not sexy enough, and that I could not hold on to my husband because I was not able to perform the way he wanted me to. I also spent many nights pretending I was so sleepy, just so I wouldn't have to make love to him. Remember, in my mind, sex was a nasty thing.

My first experience with sex was violent and very painful. There was nothing enjoyable about it. I remember the fear of having to protect myself every night, and having to sleep outside on the roof as a child. When you try to move forward into your adult life, the fears follow you. Those fears followed me into my marriage, and they were a painful reminder of my past. Nighttime for me, was like having a nightmare. You cannot tell your mate what you are feeling or what you are going through, so you try to pretend that things are fine. You have sex out of duty and loyalty, not out of love. At this point, I still didn't know what real love was all about. There were time when things were good. Then there was the burden that every time we came together, I ended up pregnant. This brought more stress to the marriage. In my mind that meant we had to be more careful and have less sex. That didn't work either; we had less sex, but six children. How many children would we have had if we had been together more?

All the time I spent protecting myself from hurt was causing more hurt in our marriage. I was not interested in sex, so I did whatever I could think of to keep from performing in that area. I would go to bed early and make sure I was asleep by the time my husband came home. Sometimes I would tell him, "I am so tired, not tonight," anything to make him mad so he wouldn't want to even look at me, then maybe he wouldn't want sex. After all that pretending, the devil brought guilt, because I knew I should have given him what he needed. In my mind, the devil showed me other women that would love to do anything he asked, and there I was—I wouldn't do the simple things needed to satisfy my husband's needs; and I said I loved him?

You live with guilt, you live with fear, and all the pain you are causing your mate because of these emotions makes them wonder whether you really love and want them; they begin to feel like they are doing something wrong. Little by little, you are teaching them to live with your fears and guilt, and to be defensive—always keeping their guard up for one of your emotions. Your spouse may have been raised totally different from the way you were raised. They may have had a complete family that shared their love and feelings with freedom. Your spouse may not understand that you feel like you are in a prison with no way out. I didn't learn about the love, sharing and freedom of expressions that should be shared between a husband and a wife in the beginning. I needed a lot of counseling before I married anybody, but I didn't have it; but I know that God has shown us a lot of mercy. There were many times I cried because I thought I was going to lose my husband if I didn't start being a better wife. It was not that I didn't want to be what he needed, I just could not do any better at that time. He took me as I was, and always told me I was the prettiest girl he ever saw. He said the first time he ever saw me, God told him I would be his wife. He said he told his mother he had met his wife, but had not really met me yet. I was the new girl in town. I met my husband when we came to North Carolina for the summer to visit with my dad. My mother said she could not handle us anymore. After the summer visit in Carolina, I wanted to stay, but my sisters wanted to go back. For me, going back was out of the question. If I would have gone back, I would have been a nut case. The Lord gave me a second chance for a new family, and a new life, and I could not mess this up. Every day I thought, "If I mess this up, I will have no where to go." This was as normal as my life had become as a child, and now there I was as an adult, not able to perform in the role of wife, a role that I had chosen. The devil tried to destroy our marriage, and he really didn't have to work very hard, but my husband and I held on to each other. I believe the reason my husband got a night job was so he wouldn't have to be rejected anymore. I was satisfied with his absence because I could sleep at night without the struggle. In the day time I honestly was too busy because of the children. This made it easier for me because it reduced the stress of having to perform sexually. Then the devil really started playing games with us. He was sending men to my husband who were having affairs on their wives. My husband was with one of these men a lot and the devil was setting him up. My husband would pick up this man for work in the morning, and when they got off, he always had places to go and things to do, which kept him from coming home. He would tell me how he had to drop this man off at a motel and then go back and pick him up. Because I knew I was not taking care of my husband's needs, the devil was having a field day with my mind. I was being tormented day and night, because taking care of his needs still seemed like a "duty". The devil was telling me, "Yeah, he finally got smart and got him another woman." "If his friend is doing it, then he is too." My husband was buying new clothes for work, looking good, and there I sat with the children. Then, the Lord sent someone to me to tell me I was pretty, and someone to pay attention to me. I needed that attention, even with what I had been going through in my emotions. When the devil sets you up he does it so that he can totally destroy you. But when God sets you up for victory, the devil doesn't have a chance.

The devil doesn't have a chance as long as you are working with the Lord.

Yes, that day came when a young man came into our lives. He needed us and at the time we thought we could help him. Not knowing what the devil had planned for me, we agreed and let him move in. He was funny and lively played with the children which gave me a break. And of course my husband worked at night and that was fine at first. Then an accidental meeting in the hall going to the bathroom happened. He began to woo me and then the affair began. It wasn't what I wanted it just happened, the devil is a opportunist, he waits for the right moment to move in. I'm not making any excuses for my action, but I was wrong for allowing it to happen. After it happened it was the excitement that kept it going. Excitement of not getting caught, but that soon came to an end when we got caught, as so many do. The enemy's plan was for all of us to die that day. Later on my husband told me the voice in his head was kill to them and then yourself, that's how the devil works. But if you resist the devil then he has to flee.

The very thing I dreaded was coming to past, I'm about to lose everything. The bible say's if you confess your sins, and repent, he will forgive you. And that old things will past away and all things are made new. That's what happened in our marriage over time. We worked hard and believed God for a change. That has made me seek after God more. I thought I knew the Lord, after that I knew I needed more of God than what I had. Thank God I found the real thing. Needless to say my husband was hurt very deeply but God has restored everything the devil tried to destroy. The enemy doesn't stop trying to take you back where you were. My husband has his own story, but he resisted the devil and won. *James 4:7 says resist the devil and he will flee.*

Now I had to learn to trust in man and God. Trust is something I needed to learn. *Matthew 6:34 Seek ye the kingdom of God and his Righteousness and all these things shall be added to you.*

Psalm 37:3 Trust in the Lord, and do good: Dwell in the land, and feed on his faithfulness.

Psalm 37:4 Delight yourself also in the Lord, and he will give the desires of your heart.

Marriage is built on trust and when you break that trust many couples don't survive. We survived because of God and loving mother-in-law who was there with words of wisdom that helped us to see that there's nothing new under the sun. The devil has played this game for ever and has succeeded but we still had a choice not just for us but for our children. She was such a blessing to me because she didn't come with blame but with real love for me, her daughter in law. We have now been happily married for thirty-four years.

ALL THINGS WORK TOGETHER FOR GOOD

The Lord takes everything and every situation in our lives and uses them to make us what he intended for us to be from the beginning. The past does hurt, and it is an embarrassment to the whole family, but God still kept us together —as a family. Through it all, I learned to trust in Jesus. This chapter was very hard for me to write because it was not just about me. The devil was telling me that I was hurting my husband because everyone knew him as a minister of the gospel at our church—what are people going to say? Well, if they have anything to say, it will be thank you Jesus. We are free and that is the most important thing; no more hiding. The story is out and the devil cannot hurt me with it anymore. The Lord has finally made me complete. I feel so clean and happy; this is the best thing that has ever happened to me. I am looking forward to all the things in life that I missed out on, and I know God will repay. I am looking forward to the devil having to pay double for the trouble he has caused us.

The Bible say's Romans 8:28: And we know that all things work together for your good to those who love God, to those who are the called according to His purpose.

Psalm 25:12: who is the man that fears the Lord? He will teach in the way chooses.

*Psalm 86: 11 teach me your ways O Lord,
I will walk in Your truth:
Unite my heart to fear your name.*

A Father And A Friend

I can remember talking about marriage with different people, but most of all, I remember talking with my pastor and his wife. They talked so openly and freely, and with so much compassion and love, it was unreal to me. I used to wish I could be like that. I wished I could live like that—seeing people express love so openly. These people were genuine; they were for real, but many times I felt so uncomfortable when people asked me questions pertaining to love and open expression. If they did ask, I would avoid answering at all costs. I could sense my husband was uncomfortable being with the brethren of the church, and they began to talk about the situation, as all men do. You never know what kind of emotions people are hiding, and those people might not be able to tell you. As you can see, I was teaching my husband how to hide also, and he didn't know it.

My pastor and his wife began teaching me about affection in a marriage. My pastor is a very special person. He has taught all of us to be open with our feelings and to express them to each other. He would always tell me he loved me. At our first meeting I thought, "This man likes women," but I soon learned that he sincerely loved all people—men, women and children. This kind of love was different from anything I had seen, in anybody, in my life. My husband's first thought was, "This man is going to be my friend," and indeed, he has been just that to us. He has been a father, friend, pastor, and everything we needed God allowed him to be that, and more. For sure, he taught us the Word, and that is why I am free today. He didn't hold back anything concerning God's Word. He didn't spare the word for our feelings, but gave it straight to us; bit by bit, God started changing us and tearing down walls in our lives. God has been good to me. I could have ended up in the wrong church, and could have gotten worse; I would have been a real mess.

The ability to be obedient to the man of God, and to be humble, was there from somewhere; that seed stuck with me, and I am thankful. Those qualities helped me go through many things in my life. If my pastor told me to do something, then no matter how difficult it was for me to do, I would do it. I am not trying to be anything except what God has created from the mess I was in. It is not for show. My prayer is that someone can be changed and set free, and that others will come out and be made whole.

Learning How To Pray

Sister Speight has made a difference in my life, especially when we started holding women's prayer. She suggested the ladies read the book, "What Happens When Women Pray," by Evelyn Christenson. Later, she took us to her home and taught us how to pray—how to get in God's presence and wait on Him. She taught us how to get to the place where God was. At first, I was very uncomfortable being alone with God. I felt like God could look through me and see that hiding person that was so bad. I don't even think the people that God put in my life even knew all that I was going through, but God gave them what I needed. I believe God was saying, "One day I am going to bring her out and she is going to be mine."

I learned how to get in the secret place with God and I found out that I could tell Him anything and He would still love me, Cathy. God used the things in the books Sister Speight gave me to read to bring change to my life. In the beginning, I was just going through the motions of being saved, not expecting God to really do anything. In my mind, I had to be good enough to earn what was already mine by the blood that Jesus shed for me. I could have stayed in that place, and would have died and gone to heaven. But God's plan had much more for me than I could have imagined. In order for God to use you the He wants to, you must be able to pray that God's will be done, and not yours. That is what I prayed, because I didn't want my will to lead my life.

Our change didn't come overnight, it came with time and patience. We had been placed into very capable hands of ministers of the gospel, who shaped and molded us into people of God—people that God can use. That is a great honor for me, and their rewards shall be many.

Coming Out Of The Cave

Every time I think about hiding, my mind sees a deep cave, dark and cold, and I am all balled up inside, shaking and afraid to come out. It is dark, so no one can find me, but God is there. The Lord began to show me that after things begin to quiet down in our lives, the hider will come out for a peek, just to look around, but we don't want to be noticed. That is how a saved hider feels. There are times we feel great and things seem to be all right, so we come out for a peek. But each time we trust God just a little, He goes into our secret place and closes up a portion of the cave; and when we come back to that familiar place, we do not have as much hiding space as we did before. The cave has become a little tighter to get into, and after a while, we long not to be there. At that time, God will allow us to sit outside, just looking and wishing we could get involved. This desire soon becomes a need to get involved, and it becomes harder to just sit looking and wishing and not participating. The need becomes more than the fear that has bound you up for so many years. Once you begin to taste and see that the Lord is good, the next time, you want a bigger taste and a bigger drink—soon you want all you can get.

Finally, I found God in a place where he talked with me and I talked with him openly. God showed me he was concerned about everything about me. I began to trust Him. I learned to trust God through the teachings of my Pastor, Dr. Anthony Speight. He has always been faithful to teach the Word, no matter how much it might hurt. Many times I was cut-up by the Word, but he kept on teaching and praying. He is a man that loves God and God's people. He has given so much to me and my family, and I know if God had not lead us to Livingway Christian Fellowship Church, my life would have been a mess. My husband and I moved to Florida, where we first met Pastor Speight. We daily submitted to God's plan and became obedient to the man of God, but our families thought we were crazy for moving. God told us to go, so we went with what we had. My husband gave up his job and we came to Florida with a car that we had to pull over at every corner, just to put oil and water in it. We said, "God if this is you, then take us there." We put gas in the car and drove all the way from North Caroline to Florida, and we have been here ever since. God has done things in our lives that will last through the next generation. God has our future in his hands and He's not finished yet. If we have the desire, God will take us all the way.

Benefits Of Coming Out

The first thing I realized was that I felt so clean. My mind was clearer than it had ever been. Finally, I knew where I was going and to whom I belonged. God told me He made me a complete woman. If you have never been torn up, you cannot know what it feels like to be made whole again. It was like I walked out of an old shell and into a new light. Things around me were bright and hope was alive. I thought this feeling would only last for a few minutes, but every minute made me want more and more of the same. These feelings were different from anything I could imagine. I guess it was like someone going into surgery and being told they were not going to make it, but after surgery, they woke up and realized they were still alive; but with no pain, only joy and peace and an assurance that it was over. Now, all I long for is to see Jesus and to see all men, women, and children delivered and free to worship God—not ashamed of anything in life. That is why we were created. Our lives should be a testimony to set someone else free. I refuse to worry; for once in my life I am sure that God can and will take care of me, without a doubt.

Well, this is the story of how my life has been. Your life may not have been like mine, but are you hiding from something? Will you come out? It is your choice. It is not over for me. Changes are still taking place and there are many more things that God is working on in me, but this area of my life is not in front of me, nor behind me, nor hidden anymore. It is out, and I am free. It may seem that I keep saying I am free, but if you had been bound like I was, and then you were set free, you would be saying it over and over again, too.

CHANGE IS A PROCESS

The cave in my life had become a safe place; a place of shelter and refuge for me. Inside it was dark with only a glimmer of sun light passing through; it was cold and damp; the ground was hard as the world outside, but it was safe because no one could find me there. I could hide for hours, or even days, but this place was imaginary; it was in my mind. I've never been inside a cave, but that place would come alive in my mind when things got heavy for me on the outside. A lot of people live in this place. I could go there now, except that God has already delivered me from that place, and I can no longer fit inside.

Many people are afraid of change. People create comfort zones; places where they can hide out and not face life or the truth. Some people get lost in television—watching somebody else act out the person they would like to be. Some people get lost in music—for hours, listening to songs with words that mean them no good. The Lord has declared that all those dark places have been covered by the Blood of Jesus Christ. I did try to go back. That's when I found out that I didn't fit anymore. Now I'm on the outside. The hidden places in my life have been exposed; and when darkness has been exposed, it cannot be used for that purpose anymore. Well, that's what happened to those old run and hide places I had; they cannot be used anymore because I don't fit there anymore.

Releasing The Past

While change is in progress, something might happen, or be said, to trigger your mind and actions about a past event. I remember when I went back home for the first time; it had been more than fourteen years. When I stepped onto those grounds, all the feelings and thoughts from all those abusive situations came rushing over me, just as fresh as the day they happened. I had no place to run and hide, and no one to tell, even though I wouldn't have told anyone if I could. The train I arrived on hadn't left the station, and the moment my feet touched the ground, every bit of the fear, anger and hurt from my past rushed over me. That was the beginning of my change. I remember it because I was so afraid; I felt like that helpless child I used to be for all those years.

I must tell you it took me a total of 38 years before my complete deliverance. My prayer is that it won't take that long for you. You see, we couldn't talk about such things when I was growing up, and even though I had been saved for 6 years before my change started to come, I still could not talk about my past. I believed that once you got saved, old things were past away and all things would become new. I still believe that, but when there are places that are hidden, God cannot heal those places until we confess them— until we open them up and expose them. I asked God one question, "Why so long Lord?" and that's when God started revealing these things to me. The Lord let me know that without confession, there is no healing; and if you live a life of hiding, it makes you think you don't have to, or need to confess anything.

It is easy to hide when you can pretend that your life is fine and that you don't have any issues to deal with. On the outside, you learn how to look and act normal, but all your associates are saying, "She's nice, but there's something else going on." You know they have questions in their mind, but you are not able to explain, so like me, you become a professional hider, and just keep to yourself. You may want to believe your situation is over, but only God knows where the road begins and ends concerning deliverance from your past. It's like that train I was riding home. It had a beginning point and a destination. Here's an example of how it was revealed to me: "When God starts you out, it's for the whole ride. The destination is already set; the tracks have been laid many years before the train starts the trip; God just needs you to let Him put the gear in drive, and you must let go of the brake. The conductor has directions for his destination. What he doesn't know about is the storm that has already started way down the road. Sometimes there is no warning of what's ahead, but the conductor knows he has to get the people on his train to their destination, as close to arrival time as possible."

I prayed and asked God for deliverance, even though I didn't know what I would have to go through to receive it; but I had a sincere heart and all intentions to live for God, no matter what it took. God already knows about the storm ahead and He knows what to do. People like me have to learn to trust. God is not blind or deaf; He knows what road you've been placed on. He knows your beginning and your end. If your train turns right or left, it is because the tracks have already been laid. If it takes a detour, then God has set an alternate route for you; but the next time that train has to come that way again, it may go straight through without detouring. Every crossroad leads back to the main track. It may take a little more time for some, than for others, but believe me you will get back on track. Every time I messed up, God was there to meet me; He was there with the answer. Sometimes it was not the answer I wanted to hear, but it was the right answer. Hiders find it hard to follow and trust God without question, because they have learned not to put their whole lives in any one's hands to make all the decisions for them. This was one of the beliefs I developed in order to protect myself.

There are many words that describe hiding: keep secret; to obscure; undeveloped; unseen; dormant; concealed, inactive; disguise; mask; suppress; withhold, veil; screen; camouflage; shroud; cover, and many of them applied to my life. Being able to admit it was a big step in the right direction for me, and today, just sitting in this big place alone writing—that's a big step for me also. For a long time I didn't know I was afraid to be alone, and I didn't know why. God revealed many things and answered many questions. Every time I get in a situation that makes me want to run and hide, but I stand and face it, God gently tells me, "See, you have overcome this again."

GOD WILL DO A COMPLETE WORK

In the process of completing the work, God takes away all of your old familiar friends: fear, pride, mood swings, lack of confidence, lack of self-respect, lust, self pity, emotional roller coasters, stubbornness, rebellion, defensiveness, self defeat, doubt. He replaces those negative things with His Spirit, in a new and positive way. I have more confidence than I have ever had, only because I know that God has everything in control. It was a long journey. God has turned me around, brought me back to Him, and set me up for completeness. Only God could do that task, but I had to be willing to participate. There were times when I was not willing to participate; those were the times when I doubted God and let fear get the best of me. But God is faithful, even when we are not. It took me 36 years to get here. I thought I was not going to make it, but I am still here.

I thank God for all the things that I have learned, but you can change today. You do not have to struggle as long as I have; you do not have to wait another minute. Open your heart and believe with your heart. God dwells with us in the secret places of our hearts. Psalms 44:21 says, "Shall not God search this out? For he knoweth the secrets of the heart." The confidence that God has given me is that all good things are coming my way. If God has plans to use you, the devil cannot stop those plans. I Peter 5:10 says, "But the God of all grace, who hath called us unto his eternal glory by Christ Jesus, after that ye have suffered a while, make you perfect, stablish, strengthen, settle you." Now, I am on a new mission to get everyone on the outside of their hidden fears and dark places in the cave. Step out and be healed.

CPSIA information can be obtained
at www.ICGtesting.com
Printed in the USA
BVHW071037150621
609528BV00003B/602